THE SINGERS I PREFER

Poems by Christian Barter

THE SINGERS I PREFER

Poems by Christian Barter

CavanKerry❦Press LTD.

CavanKerry Press Ltd.
Fort Lee, New Jersey
www.cavankerrypress.org

Library of Congress Cataloging-in-Publication Data
Barter, Christian, 1969–
    The singers I prefer : poems / by Christian Barter.— 1st ed.
        p. cm.
    ISBN 0-9723045-4-1
    I. Title.

PS3602.A8386S56 2005
811'.6—dc22
                                        2004027980

Cover Art: *The Two* © 1962 by Daniel Miller
Author Photograph by Kate Goshorn
Cover and book design by Peter Cusack

First Edition
Printed in the United States of America

Acknowledgments

I thank the following magazines for
originally publishing the following poems:

The *American Scholar*: "Another Burning," "The Way Things Look in Slides"
The *Friends of Acadia Journal*: "There Are No Stars Tonight but
Those of Memory"
The *Georgia Review*: "The Singers I Prefer," "The Two"
Interpoezia: "The Brest-Litovsk Treaty,"
"A Selection of Weapons Captured . . ."
The *Louisville Review*: "This Life"
The *Nebraska Review*: "The Last Non-Word"
The *North American Review*: "Band Camp"
The *Notre Dame Review*: "The 24th Motor Machine Gun Battalion"
"The Lost World of the Aegean," "Otherworldly"
Tar River Poetry: "Two Insects"

CavanKerry Press is grateful for the support it
receives from the New Jersey State Council on the Arts.

for Sydney Lea

Contents

Foreword by Sydney Lea   ix

PART I

The Singers I Prefer   5
Poem   7
Band Camp   9
The Two   12
Another Burning   14
This Life   15
The Deep-Sweet Way that Gods Are Sad   16
On Hearing that You Feel Bad After
    Having Sex with Me   18
Ignorance   20
Poem for the End of the World   22
Otherworldly   24
Thirty-Two   25
Could It Be Madness, This?   27
The Short Happy Life   28

PART II

Russian Dead in No-Man's-Land, 1915   33
The 24th Motor Machine-Gun Battalion
    Being Inspected, 1917   34
The Brest-Litovsk Treaty   35
A Selection of German Weapons Captured by the Canadians
    in Their Advance to Cambrai, 1918   36
The Way Things Look in Slides   37
The Exhausted Dead   39

George Dorr's Abandoned Bicycle Path   40

On a Beethoven Cello Sonata   42

Listening to Copland   44

Bach's "Unaccompanied"   46

The Lost World of the Aegean   48

Why So Few Name Their Children for the Greeks   50

What Happened   51

Blessed   53

The Things I Thought Would Save the World   54

The Irish Airman   58

There Are No Stars Tonight but Those of Memory   59

PART III

The School Bus   63

The Women at the Wal-Mart Pharmacy   65

A Room with a View   67

Shame   68

Last Putt of the Summer I Was Twenty-Nine   69

The House   71

The Last Non-Word   74

Two Insects   76

Drawing   79

Morning after Your Leaving   80

The Birds Have Just Begun   81

Almost Ready   82

The Bridge   83

Can You   85

Something Else   86

Foreword
The Cartography of Human Loss: On the Poems of Christian Barter

I am honored to introduce the stunning new poet Christian Barter, and especially to be the dedicatee of his *The Singers I Prefer*. That latter kindness owes itself to my having championed his work since his graduate student days; but, as every teacher knows, there's no magnanimity involved in supporting work of the highest quality.

Of what does that quality consist in Barter's enterprise? There is, of course, no single, simple answer. But one can infer, from the very title onward, that here is an author in grand command of what we so loosely name verse's "musical" properties.

That command doesn't manifest itself so baldly as it sometimes does in writers of formal poems. For the most part, if not always, Barter's is rather the elegance, endurance, and spontaneity of the great improvisatory performers. In the aptly titled "Band Camp," for example, I'm reminded of a player like Sonny Rollins, who can ring more "changes" on one melodic figure than the ear can quite count yet never lose touch with the figure itself. Similarly, in "Band Camp" the opening sentence stretches over 24 lines in a sinuous marvel of subordination, all the while preserving the integrity of every one of its six quatrains and each one's relevance to the entire composition.

Again and again, Barter offers us this extraordinary nimbleness and suavity, which dramatize a keen sensibility's efforts to stay just ahead of everything that threatens to dull or even to kill it—and all this, more often than not, by way of tracing what Barter calls, in "Thirty-Two," "the cartography of human loss."

In the music camp poem, the poet renders—poignantly, persuasively, typically—the inevitable compromise of our youthful assumptions and aspirations. Recalling those boyhood days, Barter cannily surmises that he had "not yet learned the scales." And few contemporaries I can think of, and certainly no first-book poet, so deftly and movingly examine the restless and unnameable desires that survive the learning of those existential scales.

Such a postlapsarian world is the one, needless to say, that all of us adults inhabit in one measure or another. Modern and "postmodern" theories abound to account for this fallenness, many of them blaming the rootlessness of industrial and, now, of technological existence. I don't necessarily quarrel with these premises, though privately I imagine our odd longings to have existed since the dawn of time: the Hebrew myth of Adam and Eve's transgression is, metaphorically at least, every bit as sophisticated and relevant to our time as the trendiest import from la belle France.

Nothing after all had changed in the world of that couple in Genesis . . . except for their consciousness of the world, and hence their selfconsciousness. Which is to say just about everything. Listen to Barter in this connection:

> My God but it would be
> a decent life to live the life
> I live! I yearn for it sometimes
> in dreams when I am far off
> riding the shrunken boards of a ship,
> thirsting for that one green spot
> of the land that will be my home.
>
>   ("This Life")

Let me not, however, mislead anyone into thinking that the motifs of loss and confounding desire are merely personal in Christian Barter's poems. Even in those poems that feature someone named "I" as protagonist, that character is awake to the existences—enviable, pathetic, often both—of other characters.

Indeed, Part II of *The Singers I Prefer* includes a number of poems, both erudite and searingly graphic, based on world-political developments, usually disastrous ones, in the prior century. I chuckle a bit to see, for example, "The Brest-Litovsk Treaty," which began as a serious response to a less than serious bit of advice I gave Christian Barter some years ago.

I cautioned him then against writing poems that clung exclusively to the personal. Not that his work had ever been narcissistic, even in his student days, but I worried lest it become so. His would hardly be the first to fall into that pit in our time. Why not, I whimsically urged, write a poem on the Treaty of Brest-Litovsk? (I must publicly credit my friend Carl Dennis—who originally handed the very same counsel to me.) To my astonishment, Barter took up the challenge, and a fine poem ensued. I am no longer astonished that other fine ones have followed, ones that take a refreshingly broad view.

But in fact all of Christian Barter's poems do that. To return to the musical lexicon with which I began, here is a writer of real range, in all the senses of that word. His most private poem manages to limn the universal, public anxieties of contemporary life, at least contemporary male life; his more public poems manage, conversely, to imply individual, private emotions so ruthlessly buried by Great Events. (See "Russian Dead in No-Man's-Land, 1915" for an especially heartbreaking example of this latter gambit.)

As I pointed out from the first, the range is as much formal and prosodic as it is thematic: Christian Barter can pull out every stop; or he can riff with the great jazz musicians; or he can write a verse so economical that you couldn't slide a razor blade into it.

Ranginess was part of the "high quality" I saw early in this writer's career. It obtains as well in *The Singers I Prefer*, but it does so more effectively and poignantly than even I would ever have predicted.

—Sydney Lea

THE SINGERS I PREFER

Poems by Christian Barter

PART I

The Singers I Prefer

The singers I prefer are the ones
who have to struggle. Famously,
there is Bob Dylan, and Robert Plant
who might have sung lower but
didn't. And now there is this
Beth Orton who seems to be singing
through a wall. Through a wall?
I would really like to get this
right. Granted, the perfect voices
on the radio today singing the "Ode to Joy"
made me cry but I was thinking—
in between the floating, the deep
hunger of dream-memories—of deaf
Beethoven locked in his smelly room,
Beethoven who probably never had
a woman groan his name in the clutch,
scribbling each note at an audience
of clefs and inkwells. It was after her face
had been scarred in the accident, when
her mouth would only open on one
side, when it tasted of acrid medicines
and something deathlike
that I saw for the first time how
beautiful M was, how damn
funny. If not through a wall, then

through some almost crippling pain,
the kind that threatens to blot out
all the sweetness, even the bursting through
of a hundred ecstatic voices
in a pickup truck in Bangor, Maine,
in a snowstorm, after a long sadness.

Poem

With the hope yet of writing a poem this morning
I am sitting in the middle of the kitchen where
I can see from the window above the sink
the early winter light bringing the old oak
to magnificent relief and can hear
the radio's classical guitar asserting
itself and struggling to reach
doubt, and I am reading from the book
of Job: "Is there not an appointed
time to man upon earth?" and watching
a spider descend by virtue of his own
guts across that oak shining
as from another earth and touch down
on the sink divider and make
for some attractive crevice. Just
being here . . . There is no such
thing, I think as I hear now Bernstein's
drifting violin above some kind of ground
that keeps giving way, a piece
inspired by Plato's *Agathon*. Beauty
is a call to labor. With the hope yet
of writing a poem smoothing

like a coin rubbed faceless, I
watch a single crow pumping
the blue he is the absence of,
working it hard until the black
of the last trees takes him.

The Singers I Prefer

Band Camp

We were so proud of our fifths of vodka
lying next to each other in Tom's trumpet case
like two long crystals harvested
from the dark cave of high school's first three years

and while less fortunate kids fingered
over and over through that one difficult passage,
Tom and I floated around campus cracking
jokes and chatting up the prettiest girls,

the prettiest, most serious of whom was Amy,
who came up to me after with her saxophone
draped around her tan neck and decreed
that we should all "drink beers" that night—

me having used that ridiculous line when we met—
and, lo, she had already gotten some
drooling 21-year-old from town
to stack them behind a bush, and when

after a day of careening back roads
in her friend's mom's car and belting with Tom
the Doors and whatever else came to mind,
the other kids were jerking uncomfortably

to that summer's teeny-bop at the band camp dance,
Amy and I strolled beneath those genuine
college campus trees, making out
whenever we felt like it. I see that I have

descended again to loving those days, though
when I woke up in the middle of the night
remembering those two bottles nestled in the case,
I was thinking what a waste I had made

of band camp, that but for drinking, and drugs later,
and all those tan necks, I might have been
a real musician in a real ensemble, wearing
an honest-to-God bow tie, gliding

through important passages. One of those
nights, before I went back to the cave from which
I was too proud to return letters,
I snuck her into my room where

in the moonlight on clinically white bed sheets
I revealed myself as a klutzy sixteen-year-old
and she as a good Catholic. After doing
nothing of lasting importance, exhausted, half-

crazed and half as someone woken up
after a long sleep, and having no idea
what a regretful, sober man I would be
at thirty-two, I said, "I love you,"

and she said, "Do you mean it?" and I, having
not yet learned the scales, the passages
of "I don't know," said, "Yes."

The Two

on a print by Dan Miller

A hunched bird looks up
from a fish skeleton as though
he doesn't understand it.

Or, no, I'm thinking that thought now,
thinking how Dan must have felt
when his eleven-year-old daughter died,
but I, as my father actually said himself,
"don't have any idea what that would be like."

You have to see the print, I guess,
the way the sky, left
as the natural grain of the woodblock,
sweeps, hangs: a vast sky,
the inside of a tree,
the inside of a terrible heart.

Even before I knew,
it held something—if not a heart—
terrible. The eyes,
they are not shocked exactly,
but looking past or through you . . .

me, I mean. You probably
have not seen it. Nor will, perhaps.

"The Two," the print is called, should you
ever get the chance.

Another Burning

I lit a fire for the first time since last winter
and it smelled like being in love with you.

I half expected—no, that word is a lie—
I imagined, in the old way, the way

I had of imagining you when you drove up
my driveway with your books on tape

blasting away calmly about Lincoln's assassination,
that you would come charging up my driveway

in the old way, last winter's way, your tears still lingering
for Abe, you'd somehow forgotten had been shot,

and let me comfort you for some long-gone thing.
It smelled like you would, and kept right on smelling that way.

This Life

is a good life, a lucky
life in a Bar Harbor spring in
1999, where the sun
backs in the sliding glass doors and
three birds practice their solos
for the next millennium. I'm not
living in it, but this life is
good, a hand-thrown mug
of coffee tasting as thick
as the ashes of Troy, the faces
of women I've loved coming
back to this life, this good,
good life that lives in May
with birds, with a plump gray
cat sprawled in a sun patch
like the emperor of spring.
My God but it would be
a decent life to live the life
I live! I yearn for it sometimes
in dreams when I am far off
riding the shrunken boards of a ship,
thirsting for that one green spot
of the land that will be my home.

The Deep-Sweet Way that Gods Are Sad

I ran into Skip one more time after my
sister dumped him—at Amigo's, the daily
drinking place for me then which I would
dump eventually with just as much
remorse. He had blown the money
for the motorcycle accident and was,
at 35, working as a bicycle courier
with Portland kids my age, his signature
rock-and-roll-length locks kicking
up their long brown legs, the red
envelope strapped down to the rack.

In the dark of my apartment he had once
strummed "Sweet Melissa"—that elegy
for 1973—for her and me,
the sirens and the tacked-up V-8s
trapped at traffic lights, the crackhead
next door cranking up another
frenzied high to the tune of a dance mix
so insipid it could steal the taste
right out of your mouth, and I
was sad in the deep-sweet way
that gods are sad for all that will
never be. It was ten years later,

stopped in traffic, almost as old
as Skip was then, that I remembered
the way he withdrew a twenty
folded lengthwise from a shirt pocket
with the care of someone taking out
an old photo, watching it all the way
to the bar, and said, "Chris,
I'll get this round," the taste
of the sweet liquor burning an instant,
the singles stacked up by his empty glass.

On Hearing that You Feel Bad After Having Sex with Me

Well, I feel bad, too, S—
bad that my coming isn't tangled up
with Sibelius-gestures, with the hope

of finding some way to die, with
smoking and laughing all the way home, with
being rock-bottom right at last, with carrying

your stones gladly through the streets, with
a fog-lifting of Boredom Supreme, with the livening
of old houses, old poems, old

trees into soul furnishings, with
the certainty death's only reason
is to drive us apart, with

a movie-like confidence in any
conclusion, with a gentle pity
for the cashiers and janitors and CEOs

who are not us, with
a thinning down to paper all
that's touchable, with cutting

to chase after chase, with
standing alone in the rain
of my own funeral, with

beating for any war that would unrape you, with
knowing this is good, respectable work, this
screwing away the morning, cramped

on a couch while just beyond
the silence of our groans this
truceless life wages on and fucking on.

Ignorance

I don't understand it any more, this state
we call ignorance. I used to think it meant
not having learned something, like what happens
when bleach and ammonia are dumped together,
or what a Wordsworth poem can excite
inside you if you only listen, or what
happened to the Roman republic around
the time of the birth of Christ, that if we

knew these things, that if we read
the right newspapers, written by journalists
who had not been bribed in peacock feathers
to tell you that new laws designed
to re-outfit emperors everywhere were really
pushed through to clothe the orphans, then we would

know about the diamond-studded robes,
the six-year-olds deep in mine shafts bathed
in coal dust, the old people bulldozed
into the grout of their own basements by
young, pretty men daydreaming on cleavage,
we would have some idea of how many villagers
were slaughtered by dough-faced boys who would
go home to bean suppers and PTAs—

we would know that the man gone red in the face
from shouting we must bomb and machine-gun
until the storm drains run with blood
and the corpses are laid across each other
like a windthrow, and the smell of rotting flesh
is as common as commercials, claims

to be Christ's disciple, who said:
Heal the sick, cleanse the lepers, raise
the dead, cast out devils: freely
ye have received, freely give.
We would know Christ said that, and that
it was about the time that Rome became
a hereditary monarchy, speech
un-freed, the senate become a rubber-stamping
mechanism, the division of the rich and the leprous

become as irreversible
as continental drift—that if we knew these things,
from reading the right newspapers, for instance,
we'd keep the bleach and ammonia on separate shelves
and heal the sick, and cast out devils,

if we only knew how—
or so I used to believe.

Poem for the End of the World

Yesterday at sunrise there was dew
on the plastic chair in the field out back,
so I brought a dry one out and last night
when I pulled in from an outing in which
a friend had said, "I've finally figured out
that girls just want to have fun," they were sitting
together, examining the moon. The world
just seems to go on functioning so well
without me, which is why I had been quiet
at the West Street that night while Eden
smiled at Mike's parody of an old drunk
who hitchhikes to the clam flats
every tide with his twelve-pack, and John
having recently learned what women want,
caressed a bruise on a girl's thigh while her breasts
contemplated the ceiling. "The Four Horsemen,"
the bartender explained to a patron
who had asked about the name of a drink,
"were War, Famine, Pestilence,
and Death." "I meant what's in it," the patron
muttered, not particularly interested
in the end of the world, and I thought of pointing out
that after the other three, Death
was a little redundant. But it seemed a shame
to disturb them. His name

was Jerry, the clam digger, and once
when I picked him up he had a moment
of insight between swills of Bud and said,
"I don't fucking know, man." "Me neither," I said,
and he looked at me as though he had forgotten
I was in the truck with him, working the pedals and the wheel.

Otherworldly

Otherworldly—and not simply because this was
a dream—you stood, hovered, in the great halls last night,
seventeen again and I that mix of souls we seem
to manage properly only in the deepest part
of sleep. Not simply because this was a dream
did I suggest we do it real this time,
as adults do it—not the sex, which we
had nailed down well enough by the time you turned
twenty, rowing yourself home on my
scull-like torso—but the house, the promises,
the unforeseen. How easy they make it seem
to be alive, these dreams, to simply find
in the great halls somewhere, you, and act
according to the obvious need. Not at all
like the night we stood at the overlook
at that age when the instinct of hope begins to battle
with details such as the ending of summer, you
going back again. "I thought about asking you,"
spoke out one soul, trying to interpret the thoughts
of another soul, and you said, "Oh, Christian,"
putting a name on both. And that was it—
for Planet Earth, anyway—
and not simply because it is a dream.

Thirty-Two

                              and I think I understand less,
seeming to be standing, as it were,
away from whatever gases I was breathing
a decade or so ago. More, probably,
about avoiding pain, about
drinking enough fluids and looking
closely at the ground, but I was
wiser as a hormone-wracked
hitchhiker on an unmapped road. I knew,
for instance, that fun and eternity
existed, that I was intended by
the universe, and even a little something
about quantum theory, which I couldn't
answer a single question about
the other day when it leapt
into that valence shell called "work."
An elaborate complaint, I know,
but if there's one thing I've learned it's that
squeaky wheels are better than none
and at thirty-two it's better,
as Machiavelli sort of said, to be
feared than fucked because then
your island won't go for trinkets
and you might even get a morning now and then
to memorize a line or two of Lear's before

you get there yourself: *Oh, fool I shall go mad!*
Wisdom is the bone that's left
when the other stuff has rotted: the stuff
about Kim being magically across
the room stretched on a couch while Dylan
predicts in a smoky ecstasy the boredom
to come: *You gonna make me lonesome*
when you go, and the stuff about
the taste of a cigarette when the world
was as whole as Pangea, before
the Big Bang, The Light, The Word. I know
these are old clichés, but so am I now,
a bald man with a vendetta and a tool box,
and one or two crash courses below his belt
in the cartography of human loss:
ten paces from the tree, that sort
of thing. That apple core
must be around here somewhere.

Could It Be Madness, This?
—Emily Dickinson

The world has so many ways of fooling us and maybe
if the soul is dispensable and love is a combination
of chemicals and electric jolts it doesn't
matter much. Otherwise, it's offensive, the number
of songs that pretend M is back, these dreams
of coastal, windowed houses imbued with the depth
of that world that looks as this one, but has no
traps and what's good goes on and on. Which
is it, friend, impostor? Of course we will get
nowhere with this discussion, and after it forgets us
my grandmother will still be dying in Ames, Iowa,
anticipating the next drawing out of fluid
from her cancered lungs, and Sarah McLaughlin
will still be singing, using every word
she knows, *It goes on, it goes on, it goes on.*
Could it be madness, this?
It goes on, it goes on, it goes on.

The Short Happy Life

It was "The Short Happy Life of Francis Macomber"
that finally got my attention,
reading Hemingway the night before the exam,
trying to scan, pick up plots and names,
and thus slide through the way I'd slid
through everything, the way I'd keep on sliding
years past that through shit jobs, girlfriends,
windowless rooms and bars. It simply hit me
what Hemingway was talking about. There's a man
on safari in Africa or someplace who
suddenly finds his courage when he's
confronted by a charging water buffalo—
at forty or something—and I felt
that I would someday find my courage
too, drinking a six-pack to calm those finals jitters.
I had been the kid the tough kids jeered,
and stole his hat, and called a fag,
and beat up now and again, though
never that bad. The beatings are never
that bad, and they come anyway, which is what
this guy of Hemingway's realized after he
had cowered in the face of some other animal
and his wife snuck back to the tent from
fucking the guide. The beatings are going
to happen. I failed the class and hid

behind the library smoking cigarettes
while my classmates marched. Macomber's wife
blew his head off, seeing that he'd leave her,
and Hemingway blew his own head off. I don't know
what *he* saw coming, if he was scared, or just
bored. But that night my finals meant nothing.
I was living my own short happy life.

PART II

Russian Dead in No-Man's-Land, 1915

Someone cobbled with care the soles
that now face us of these boots built
to the knee. Someone kept this white hat
spotless. Someone trimmed,
not long ago, the hair
of these two twinned by death, carefully
short around the ears to turn out lice.
Someone handed out these pants, and if
they were not quite right for dying in,
accepted them back and handed out
another pair, seamstressed
by sure Russian fingers. Someone fixed
this bayonet to this rifle stuck in the ground.
Someone penned the letters crammed
deep in the handsewn, resewn pockets.
Someone imagined them.

The 24th Motor Machine-Gun Battalion Being Inspected, 1917

We have gotten so used to things that kill that it
may take a moment for the utter absurdity
of these machines to sink in: primitive
motorcycles with exposed intestines and old-lady
handlebars, mounted with machine guns on one side
and one of those squeeze-ball horns on the other
that clowns pull out of polka-dot pants. Not
a smile among them however, these men who stand
as erect as the war's last year will let them,
hands clasped behind, between the row on row
of Wizard-of-Oz machines parked
straight as gravestones. They cannot see
the sleek jets darting over Iraq as I
write this poem, casually demolishing
from the stratosphere one-well towns.
They cannot see themselves.

The Brest-Litovsk Treaty

Trotsky and Joffe, ever-intellectual in those
little round glasses that have lately come back into rage,
rolling to the treaty table in the back of a great,
open car on a brisk Brest-Litovsk morning,
Joffe with one arm propped on the side, as people
do now in Boston and Prague, studying
the camera's lens that has lately become this writer,
Trotsky slunk in an upturned collar, a man
amused by deconstructionism
in an L.A. bar, his Charlie Chaplin
bowler the only reason to suspect
these are otherworldly men sent forth
from a pitchforked empire—and now we can begin
to guess at what they might be willing to sign.

A Selection of German Weapons Captured by the Canadians in Their Advance to Cambrai, 1918

If you had taken in like a tourist
the rest of the book's photos,

of course this is what would be left:
neat rows of guns in the dust

of old film. Meticulously laid,
they round a corner and blur

into a dark thicket, from which only
the cannons in back are still

recognizable, their long necks
craning to see the next cathedral.

The Way Things Look in Slides

As though pierced through with light,
the living hearts in the extinguished room,
an exotic jungle of green in each leaf—

the faces, even the faces of the very old,
of those who have lost too much,
basking in the light, the sky

shocking in its concentrate of blue,
or a faintly glowing mist become
a way of life the dead branch reaches into.

It's going there all at once, of course,
that does it, surprises you
into seeing the world as it really is:

pierced through with light. That is why,
more than you were alive today
you are with your father thirty years ago

as he takes a shower in Vietnam,
the water cascading over his
muscular shoulders, his head tipped back

in exquisite relief as he mugs for the camera
in a forest so luxuriously beautiful
it almost wants for restraint,

where death has been rubbed out
with a portion of the sky and now
it is clear that we have always been in heaven.

The Exhausted Dead

Better, I say, to break sod as a farm hand
for some poor country man, on iron rations,
than lord it over all the exhausted dead.
                                        —Achilles

Ah, yes. And where have all your taxing exploits
landed you, you who once were looked upon
as an immortal god? Not you, Achilles,
dead in a long-closed kingdom of the dead,
but you: reader, self. What speck of good
has it done you that once on summer streets
you were so beautiful carfuls of girls
stopped to coax you inside? Toward what end
did you drink whisky to Springsteen's elegies
with the friends who loved you all of those July
afternoons, so beautiful and so slow
to tire, with so much night ahead? What help
to you now, the bronze women you worshipped,
the mornings you slipped to a strange street, her scent
around you like a highly fashioned shield . . .
you, who once were looked on just as a god—
not you, Achilles, dead in a long-closed kingdom,
but you, reader, self? Better, I say—
all of us say it's better to break sod.

George Dorr's Abandoned Bicycle Path

They say it may have been—built
in 1906—the world's first
trail for mountain biking, now all
the rage for the synthetic-garbed,
the nuclear-bright, those young

as Dorr himself was then,
and as rich. What's left of the loop
is a few unflooded yards behind
a beaver pool, as plain as Day-Glo,
the massive stones along the sides

still cradling, a hundred years later,
the old gravel. Forgotten
by the glaciers first,
it came from the hollow pits
in the hillside where now

you might think meteors had landed,
a wheelbarrow-push away, before
there were backhoes and front-end loaders
and excavators, and D-8 dozers.
I have seen the pictures,

the women in their layered, long dresses
and flower-garden hats, standing
with their one-speed bicycles, frowning
as people in old photos do,
as though they disapprove of what

we did with their lives, the landscape
unrecognizable, before
the fire, the Loop Road, the puffing
laboratory now always in view. Only
the path looks familiar,

a column in a long-gone, jungled
wilderness into which they might have
ridden away, had those bicycles
had twenty gears and full suspension,
had their legs been free.

On a Beethoven Cello Sonata

I.

What would this cello be saying
if cellos could speak? But that
is a silly question; it is already
muttering behind, soaring over
in sudden realization, conversing
matter-of-factly with the piano,
which is clearly the timid one,
the one who makes excuses for his
outspoken friend, restates things
ironically, without emphasis, that we
might remember them as being
something less than the heartbreaking
visions of a mad soul. Listening
to this sonata, we may realize
that the thoughts we put into sentences
have no grip on us, take on
meaning only in long legato lines
that could have been made of anything, even
the scratching of a horse's hairs on his own guts.

II.

What I love about Beethoven is what
I so often hate about myself:
he never finishes anything. The strain
that labors cadence after cadence toward
resolution, wresting its course away
from the pestering piano, arrives
only after everything is so changed
that where it meant to go is no longer
possible, is there only as a memory
of where we might have rested. Perhaps
it isn't me, but life itself I hate
for this deception, though without it
(am I right about this?)
there is no beauty anywhere.

Listening to Copland

Listening to Copland I hear
the gestures that TV shows
and commercials and bad or so-so movies will be
using for the next fifty years

until I can almost see the TV-yellow
fields and see the joyous cheeks
of the dancing pioneers, the spaceship

maneuvering the asteroid belt
at the beck of model-pretty hands,
the conquest of good and wholesomeness

that will pollute forever
this strange and powerful music.

I hear the high school bands blowing
like stopped traffic. I see

men pretty as Dorian Grey in a cashmere suit
ascending marble steps
to "Fanfare for the Common Man."

I hear them quoting
Martin Luther King and naming
Jesus as a fiscal conservative.

There is so much truth that even lies are made of it.

Bach's "Unaccompanied"

I.

Why would we need to march, andante,
into the Viennese Period
and pillage its symphonies, let
alone into the year 2000,

where each of a million doorways blasts
its own overwrought mix
and everyone is talking—
a few who can't seem to talk enough
are speaking out of boxes on the walls—

Do we need all those voices? Do we need
even a piano's commentary?
For I have noticed
that many voices heard together
become a single voice, and that even

silence, after a while, will begin
to squeak in its chair, to cough.

II.

Is it thought? Or form only,
exquisite form, the thoughts
being mine, the way I think
of cliff formations, the perfect
curve of the horizon, suspended
sunset colors . . . Form only, then,
this: letter, word, line,
the thought as dead as Bach,
every bit as dead
as the sky, the cliff, the ocean
bulging toward a faint moon.

III.

Bach knew what the others guessed:
accompaniment is a ruse, and anyway,
unnecessary. Left alone,
passages begin to speak
to each other. It might
be wrong to call it "lovingly"
but loving is a ruse, and anyway,
unnecessary. Take everything away
and the nothingness, I assure you—
yes, it is you to whom I speak—
the nothingness will sing to itself.

The Lost World of the Aegean

On the cover of *The Lost World of the Aegean*,
in a pile of reading on my kitchen table,
a painting displays two Minoan women
in finely wrought jewelry feeding a monkey
between the pillars of a stone bathhouse.
Nearing the end of another relationship,
I'm at the point where
I don't want anything to die anymore—
the women, the monkey, the civilization,
even the creator of the Marlboro Man,
whose obituary photo in *Time*
is lying next to the book, a man
who lured millions to an early,
miserable death. His childish grin is lit up
in '62, sucking air and cracking jokes
just thirty-five years before being snuffed out,
oblivious to the whole idea of misery,
as I am on the refrigerator door
at 22, waving to the crowds
of the future from my new pickup,
pulling out of the driveway,
going back to Portland where I will meet
a woman I do not love who will, a year later,
have a son I will never see.
And why shouldn't he be happy?

Jack Kennedy is beaming far from Dallas,
escorting his beautiful wife
down perfect marble steps
in The Greatest Country on Earth
and new machines are going to
save us all from having to work,
perhaps, someday, from having to die.
Even the dry historian breaks down
and refers to Crete as "a lost and golden land,"
though the rest of the story is like the others:
an awakening, a series of disasters,
a pile of tablets not yet deciphered.

Why So Few Name Their Children for the Greeks

It isn't because the names are difficult
to spell, or because, but for a few, they went
from this world with their bowels hanging out,
the gorgeous armor pierced, the black swirling up,

or because, taken as a group, they'd rather
fight than fuck, set fire to someone else's
tower than build their own, hit the ocean
than potty-train a kid. It isn't because

most of their gods were one big dysfunctional family
who, in the end, were able to save so few
from Hades, where pissed-off shades hung out, grumbling,
in permanent withdrawal from the living.

And it isn't because their poets were blind, or dike-ish,
their philosophers unpopular, their jurors
comically shortsighted (but for a few, it seems),
their columns toppled, their blood-earned legends become

the stuff of yawns and fustian dissertations.
Except for a few. And now you know the reason.

What Happened

There were too many roadblocks and
not enough road. After we
got out in the forest, we realized
our map wasn't color-coded. No
oxygen. Upon closer inspection,
it turned out that beam was rotted
right at the base. A goddam
system error. It wasn't until
the iceberg was in sight that we
thought to count lifeboats. We
must have overslept.
We were talking about our
careers when I looked up and saw
the turn in the road. It was
classic. It was so sudden. She
couldn't hear me screaming at her,
what with that crash helmet on.
Have you ever heard of
Pickett's Charge? Then, the fucking
snakes were all over the place. It
was like we had become our parents.
We put the broken microwave
on the sidewalk, but no one
would haul it away. It was like,
fucking awful, man. I watched,

feeling, at first, nothing as the
casket was lowered into the mud.
We couldn't see shit.
There was this incredible wave
of heat and then people running
in all directions. The plan
was simple, but everything hinged
on that one detail. We must have
miscounted. We never did learn
how to tie the proper knot.
There was more than a single shot
fired, that much is certain. Why
would we have thought to look
under the bed? We panicked, I guess.
It was so hot under the lights,
and we hadn't slept in days. We
left the goddam sandwiches at home.
As it turns out, there
never was any gold. Then
everyone stood up but us
and started singing.

Blessed

Three days after the towers fall
I wake up to acorns knocking on the roof
and congressmen singing "God Bless America"
in barroom voices out in the yard
where my neighbor is blasting statements schooled
in serious inflection while he pounds
nails: tragedy and revenge,
a people under siege. In my barn, I count
the dead: four spiders, peacefully in webs,
a shell and legs on the windowsill, destroyed
beyond recognition, and a speckled ladybug
shining like a beach pebble, caught
in the act of commuting the work bench.
The neighbor's radio offers a sad prelude
and the oak tree goes on mindlessly shelling roofs
until one might think America
were a dream snoozed up by tired stock analysts.
I don't know what it would mean
to be blessed, if it's this rescue worker cheered on
by the crowd, who tells the reporter
without thinking, "This is beautiful,"
or my neighbor crawling back into his shell,
or the well-fed dog across the road unleashing
his frustration at cars rushing
past all day, day after day,
and not one of them a fucking rabbit.

The Things I Thought Would Save the World
(or "How I Became a Nihilist")

I. Inventions

Mine. Namely,
a rubber-band-powered car
that used no gas
and a spaceship we could all
live in when Brezhnev nuked
the Navy base the next town over.
As one rubber-band wound down
it wound another up.
This process would be repeated forever.

II. Politics

Carter/Mondale. Mondale/Ferraro.
Dukakis? I was too old
for Clinton. By that time
they all seemed
like cynics, which means, I guess,
that I had become a cynic.

III. Poetry

Dear Lord, did I?
If not the world, then
one small, imagined corner of it.

IV. Marijuana

Not this
world, necessarily, but
the real one underneath it all
on which our lives float like—
this is getting deep—
like driftwood or something. Well,
not that it needs saving, the
real world underneath it all, just
finding again and again and again.

V. Love

The anti-political-petroleum-
nuclear-urge-to-power
love, which is the overcomer—I
believed it might (by this time
I spoke of maybe's) overcome

the urge to mutilate, the drive
toward ruin of the gorgeous Roman kind.

VI. God

It had to happen sometime.
It was night and I was
grief-stricken in a ball field, begging.
I remember that everything—
the dark tree-shapes, the scattered stars—
seemed reflected in water.
And whether it was Him, or
Me, or What, I got my wish:
it was, for a time, All Right.

VII. Nothing

I began to spy it
everywhere, grinning like a skull
beneath the skin
of all I had believed, had
sung, had loved so much
that I believed it sang to me,

the world, and then
Nothing sang and it was like
nothing I had ever heard and then I
finally believed that
Nothing will save the world.

The Irish Airman

A waste of breath, those years behind,
In balance with this life, this death.

—Yeats

So sang the Irish airman and I would like to sing it too
someday letting the earth drop down out of my talons
and roll its play life beneath me. But surely Yeats's
airman was twenty-two and cramped up to the armpits
with the life, the death inside him, surely ignorant
of the comfortable wasting and the little-by-little losing cares
that comes with the days that begin to pass faster
and farther away, little cars on little roads headed
elsewhere. Surely this Irish airman still believed himself
deserving of the vast-lit sky bent taut across
the distances, of the casual love the other wasted
breathers bestowed by way of dirty jokes and the dull stories
of foreign love, deserving of the foreign love I won't
describe except to mention, in passing over, its awakening
of that inner airman like a siren, how he fumbled in frightened joy
for his cold leather. Surely this man of twenty-two
with such a gift for telling why the hopeless, with nothing
to gain, will occasionally break free of the fields
and indulge themselves in god-fights is reeling
with the pleasure of his bones, as were
we all, letting the earth drop down.

There Are No Stars Tonight but Those of Memory
—Hart Crane

Tonight the real stars seem
just memories

crowding the black above my house

still bright as any city
seen from a hill

where cities seem to be

the things we planned to build.

PART III

The School Bus

In the dream I was getting on the school bus
from the back of the bus for some reason, only this time
instead of jeers and everyone sliding over
to the aisle-side so I couldn't sit down, someone said,
"There's a seat up here, Chris." It was

next to Mary Jo Stillwell, pretty as she was
in eighth grade, who had slid to the window
to let me sit, and when a kid put me in a headlock
I simply lifted him over my head and set him
in the seat in front of me, said, "Stay there,"

and a little boy had grabbed a little girl
by the hair, only this time I pulled him off
and sat him down, saying, "You don't ever grab a girl,"
and sat her down, too, and asked her if she was all right.
No one jeered at this, or swore at me,

or threatened my life for disrupting the way things
were supposed to be on the school bus going to
Mountain View Middle School in Sullivan, Maine—
if that's even where we were going—
and when I sat back in my seat, Mary Jo leaned forward

in a very serious manner, and I kissed her
as though it were the most natural thing to do
with Mary Jo—short, serious kisses—on that
school bus that was nothing like any school bus I had ever ridden,
that was exactly like every school bus I have ever ridden,

and when she started kissing my neck in a way that tickled,
I woke up exactly in my life.

The Women at the Wal-Mart Pharmacy

Jenn has spelled her name with two
n's to draw it out longer as one might
wish to do were she thrown
all over you some morning in that
lost hour before work, the only one
here who smiles a human smile, the kind
a kid would smile as she
performs her part of this assembly line–like
process, which is asking me
my name when I have come back
to see if it's ready. The others—
well, the first one liked me well enough
before she looked up from her computer
and I became one of the sick who have kept her
from scrolling so many happy screens,
and the tired pharmacist who might be
all right, just tired, just
a little too aware she is the only one here
who doesn't dye her hair from a box—she
has been to college but never
swamped in the joy of all those
ancient, willing souls, or so I gather
from the glance she gives the futuristic
gun with which Jenn with two n's

is trying to dust-bust the label
of my pills, from the way
she says, "That reading is something like
thirty years old," which might be
funny were it not so joyless, though Jenn
just cheerfully stares into the barrel of the thing
as though it were totally harmless, all
of it, and then passes through
the stage-set door and reappears
at the cash register to hand my prop
to the woman there. This last one
is downright executionary, the way she
demands the sum and doesn't even
flinch when I joke, "My God,
really?" just stares at the debit card
in my hand as though there were
nothing ridiculous in all of this, nothing
more important, as though
there were no lost, drawn-out hours before work.
I cough, and punch the correct numbers.

A Room with a View

How fortunate, that last meeting with Mr. Emerson
in the church, how much like
an intervention—of God, or the Writer.
And that Lucy would see his meaning
and understand at last that she loved George,
and that George would not have
offed himself, or left the country, or
put himself in a deathlike trance, calling
forth the need for unreliable messengers—

this is all very fortunate. Not to mention
being born with money and good looks
and not, in that day and age, having died
or been disfigured by one or another
then-horrifying disease. I see once again

that love is for the very lucky, or else
there is some Will that will not, generally
speaking, be frustrated by details. Will you,
M, now insurmountable in your other life,
wander someday into my church, confused,
and be turned toward the life I have long imagined?
This book made it seem as though you would,
and for that, I threw it at the wall.
It's somewhere out of sight in Another Room.

Shame

There were, he supposes, some periods of time—
some moments, some days, perhaps an entire year—
in which he wasn't ashamed of himself,

when he felt as though he had landed
on the right earth after all, as though
the years of self-loathing he had heaped,

reeking, had finally broken down
into fertile soil—had been necessary,
but had finally broken down.

These are the moments, the days—
perhaps an entire year—
of which he is most ashamed.

Last Putt of the Summer I Was Twenty-Nine

for Dan Baldridge

As I'm getting up off my knees where I was going into
pro-style histrionics over a missed putt on the eighteenth,
laughing, and shouting at Dan in the evening air just cooling
that half the ball must be hanging over the edge of the hole,

I see the figure, a grim shape under the manicured trees
walking in our direction, then definitely toward us,
speaking before he reaches a comfortable distance
so that his voice surprises with its intentional clarity—

Are you folks members? The moon is a bony crescent,
bright now in the darkening blue with its craters standing out
like the ruins of lost cities, the crickets just beginning
to speak to each other in the longer grass beside the fairways

as a breeze excites to a hushed whisper the last full leaves,
hidden now in the blurry dark of their trees blending in the sky
which releases its last pink light behind them—*a perfect
summer night*, as I was prattling to Dan coming up the fairway

with our clubs thrown across our strong backs like the careless loads
of whatever loves it was we bore that summer, whatever
handicaps, the kind of night that always seems
not really over, just held up by some stickler for the rules.

The House

Jack, who plows the school, runs
with the Southwest Harbor Ambulance, goes
on calls for the Volunteer Fire Department,
calls the poker game last night after
he's left down a hundred, and Dan says,
"No, I don't think that's his house," looking
straight at me—

                                        Jack, who is still
awake at two in the morning, his scanner
blurting to "all units" its
little emergencies, who does this shit
because his mother was an alcoholic
who bought the beer for the local kids
her children's age, all of them
stoned any night of the week
in the brown synthetic living room, before

we grew up, and she blew up with cancer—

ah, fuck, who knows if that's why—

if that's why Jack says, "Yah,
whatever pal," no matter what

you tell him, why he left
his last girlfriend after the baby, why

I left a woman seven years ago,
her stomach grown hard
as a deployed airbag—where

can I lay the blame? Dan says,

"Bart, that ain't your house is it?"
so I take the phone and Jack is
unsure about the road names—

                    my
house where all the good things left
in the world are crammed: my
books, my Beethoven, my gentle
cat Waldron I found behind a log
by the side of the road, so small

he fit in the palm of my leathery,
warted hand—

                but eventually blurts out,
"Old Norway Drive," the next road up,
where I will see, driving home after
sleeping off the beer, the last

gray tufts of smoke rising
into the bright morning sky as though

a string were tugging them upward,

and I say, "Jack, thank you,"

and he says, "Yah, whatever pal."

The Last Non-Word

Miranda, on the way to get my mail
I saw two vultures drifting so near each other
I thought at first just one great bird was floating
over those tall pines standing along the bay
where Route 3 passes so close to the ocean
you can look down into its churning, where I always
feel somehow safe, observant, above it all
as it carries the islands on its long gray back.
One bird kept easing into the other one,
as though brought by a current in the air,
so unpretentiously I might have thought them
scanning for food along the road except
the pursued one began turning over, reaching out
her legs, at which point she'd begin to fall
like a soiled rag blown out of an open window,
flapping her useless dead weight toward the ground,
and have to turn upright to become again
that gracefully drifting creature. I had heard
that this is how birds of prey are forced to mate—
talons clenched, face-to-face, plummeting down—
but had never quite believed it, such a drama
fitting too well that big cliché called love.
I thought, when you left, I'd call you, begging *please*,
but I find myself grown quiet and observant
of strange, important things like this, as cars

along Route 3 roar past on daily missions.
I waited for the birds to interlock
in that love-death spiral toward the great blank ocean,
to claw, scratch, scream into the empty cliffs
and barely make it out alive, or else
not make it, let the ocean have the last
non-word. But she kept blithely righting herself
and eventually they simply flew away—
majestic, safe, that one small task postponed.

Two Insects

I.

The first one I let go because I found him
already on his back, walking the air
with all six legs. What a terrible
design. You build a car like that
and you've got a lawsuit on your hands.
But these things are disposable—they
breed by the millions and won't even
help each other up. I flipped him
with a spoon that still had some food on it
and he buried his flat head in the glob
it left as soon as he could stand. Why
waste time contemplating the last close call?
I got him back into the spoon and
tossed him out the back door, where
the morning sun was eating a tunnel
through an aging stand of spruces.

II.

The spoon that saved the other squashed
the second little guy because he had
pincers that looked positively

medieval. He was clamoring behind
the coffeemaker with the canny trepidation
of killers, who know better than anyone
how worthless our own lives are.
When I finally let up after rolling
the spoon back and forth over
his crunchy shell, his body
was a black mess but the pincers
were still intact, the part that was
built to last. On the way to the garbage
to drop him with the flies and rotting meat
I kept his corpse at arm's length.

Drawing

Many nights in a row now I've been woken up
by the past. As if it wants

to show me something with these
clayey remembrances—just now

a note from Chris McCall
on the dresser in the room we shared

in the relaxed aura of opportunity
of Bar Harbor twelve years ago

that says, "Took some of your Marbies,"
under the pack in which he'd left

one cigarette, and a drawing,
of all things, of a man's face

which I woke up thinking about,
wondering why had Chris, who never

did anything artistic other than
carp Lionel Richie after a twelve-pack

and bust out laughing, drawn that
serious-looking face? Something about

friendship, perhaps, is what it wants
to show me, or maybe the past

can't sleep either. I remember now
the nights we sat all night at the window,

sending our smoke into the street and getting
back the sweet cool of August,

our words loaded with careless
importance, as though we thought

that even our smallest gestures
would last forever.

Morning after Your Leaving

When I'm done with their questions
the tourists go back to their cars by twos,
toting their cameras.
They were looking to glimpse something
magnificent, and hold onto it,
but the peregrine falcons
who raised four chicks on this cliff,
calling each other from the peaks
of their spiraling dives,
are already gone south. Now
only trail workers hang from ropes
and dislodge chunks of granite
which tumble and bounce
like toys tossed from a crib.
I'm trying to explain
to these moralizing tourists
that sometimes rockslides just happen,
that no person is to blame
for the sudden failure of the granite face
that closed this path to the summit.
No one is listening.
Some of them want to go up.
Some of them just want to know
that it would be all right
to go up if they wanted to.

The Birds Have Just Begun

The birds have just begun
their chatter, a little before
sunrise, carrying on.
"Give it a rest," the high school kids
who work the summer
on my crew would say,
if they could talk. One
is caressing the same minor third,
that mournful interval,
over and over. He must be
the bard. The others are
more cheerful, more
cacophonous—something about
the joy of the quotidian.
They can't seem to get beyond it.

Almost Ready

I am almost ready to forget about the leak
in the ozone layer as the morning sun
hangs over the harbor, misting the water
into a mast-high translucent veil
as warblers prattle on with the racket
of mating as though this were but one spring
in eons of springs to come. Fishing boats,
like children's stick sculptures, suspend
their ropes and pulleys from booms
that ascend into the layers of the dawn,
and I am almost ready to forget
that the fish have been dragged out to feed
horizon-lengths of honking tract-house families
whose car exhaust has drifted
up the coast, hazes the mountains.
I let the line go slack on the petty workday
stretching in front of me, so lulled by waves
exhaling on the rocks that I am
almost ready to believe that this man and woman
walking the shore, picking up pieces
of broken bottles smoothed to bright stones
are seeing the harbor through the softened glass
of love, some species of love that's protected,
that it would be a kind of redemption if they were.

The Bridge

At sixteen I was killed in a car wreck,
crossing the bridge from Sullivan
where I grew up, mostly, to Hancock,
which is on the way to Ellsworth
where I'd gotten a job flipping burgers
and putting down fries. I would have
been a senior that year, developed
a drinking problem, lost
my virginity in a prefab basement
to a girl I didn't know, would never
know, gone on to an elite college
and studied the works of Hegel and
Schopenhauer and Beethoven, learned
that they were German Romantics
and not much more—due to my
drinking problem which by now
would have turned into habitual
marijuana-smoking and sleeping around.
I guess it would have been fun
for a while, living, like that.
I think I would have chosen Kim
to fall in love with, have kissed her
right there in the Roger Williams Hall
at a keg party, have helped her
with her garnet coat and walked her

home nights after starchy dinners,
fingers cinching with fingers
in the itchy wool pocket, then
drunk myself away from her
for three straight months
until I came home to a short note.
I digress. It's easy to get
carried away with things that never
happened, to get saddened by some
life that might have been, though
had I lived I probably would have
read Nietzsche, too, who said,
*What does it matter that you
are failures? How much is still
possible!* The accident was due
to driver inexperience, excessive speed.
He must have been in a terrible hurry
to get somewhere.

Can You

Can you love the dawn and hate the day? I do.
"Addicted to the beginnings of relationships,"
as I've been told. And told. And told. The new
light looks as something else when it first hits,
something more like Catherine standing up
across a strangered room, that promising look
she had before the promises, still stuck
with sweetness to her face in my notebook
of pre-day ecstasies. I love the feel
of gray seeping into black—what it represents:
the casting-out that could occur—and the real,
truant world opening, before it grows dense
with light and the need for endings, setting free
that inkling some lasting love might come to me.

Something Else

I know a woman who calls me
every week or so when she has something
on her mind and starts by saying,
"I have something to talk about
but let's start by talking about
something else." It helps her get it out.
So I ask her how she is and she says
okay and tells me about some poet
or politician she's met and how
he wasn't at all what she expected
or about the D.C. weather,
the traffic jams, the dirty Metro.
Sometimes she never gets around to her point
at all, but ends by saying,
"Now I don't want to talk about it
anymore." Last week I had a fever
for four days and the world
took on a kind of flickering darkness—
it seemed so thin, so insubstantial,
not the kind of place a person could live.
This guy who came to the card game
last night, he says he dreams
of a dead friend all the time,
this friend walks out of a black alley,
walks always in a kind of shadow.

I asked him what it's like to be dead,
the guy said, fumbling a face-down card,
and he said it's not a place, heaven,
it's a feeling, the feeling of knowing
everything you never knew. Then the friend
told him one of the numbers to play
this week in Megabucks. Sometimes, though,
she does get around to what's on her mind—
a sadness for her little sister, killed
in a wreck, or a fear that we
won't see each other again, won't ever
feel whatever that was we felt when we
were making love. I don't know if we will.
I don't know if she will ever see
her little sister again except in dreams,
which is somewhere, I guess.
The number was eight.